ANIMALS SEND Valentines TOO

By Christina & Eli Kamerow

Copyright

Animals Send Valentines Too
Illustration and Text Copyright Christina and Eli Kamerow

All rights reserved. No part of this book may be reproduced in any form or by an electronic or mechanical means, including information storage and retrieval systems, without permission in writing from the publisher, except by a reviewer who may quote brief passages in a review. Independently published by Thrifty Carrot Publishing. To contact write to thriftycarrotpublishing@gmail.com or visit www.thriftycarrot.com.

ISBN 979-8-9985441-0-1
First Edition 2025

For Wren

We all know about Valentine's Day
Where we give away hearts and cards to say
"I like you!" "You're my friend!" Maybe you have a little crush,
With chocolates and sweets, you might get a sugar rush.
But what about animals? What do they do
When they see another animal they want to be their boo?
So carry on, brave reader, and this book will show you,
That animals like to send valentines too!

Some beetles have a bioluminescent abdomen,
From North American backyards to the Great Plains African.
When a firefly's inspired by a potential mate,
A chemical reaction makes him illuminate,
As a signal to females below in the grasses -
Many species have their own style of flashes.
If the female's receptive and finds the light show impressive,
She'll copy his flashes, guiding him with directions.

La la la la la, what a beautiful tune!
A mouse whistles when it wants to find a mate soon.
Sniff sniff - when he smells a potential mate's near,
He squeaks a song too high-pitched for us to hear.
Hoping ultrasonic vocalizations
Will give the female romantic inclinations.
If interested, she might sing along and start grooving.
If not she'll run away and keep on moving.

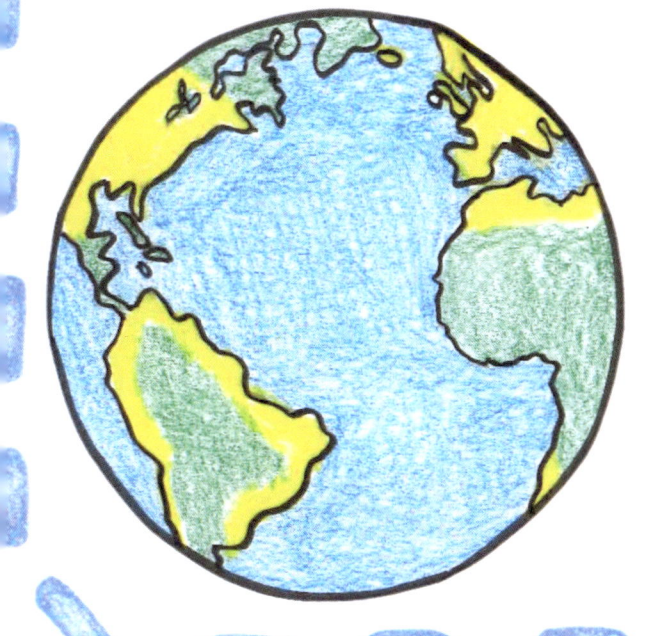

When flamingos are single and ready to mingle,
They do a group dance and hope the routine will
Impress a female by flapping their wings,
Craning their necks and honking their beaks.
If the hen is keen on the routine she's seen
She'll mirror his posture, then they clean with a preen.
All this to find the right individual!
And they dance every year, it's an annual ritual.

When a pufferfish sees another fish whose heart he wants to win,
He swims in a circle and shakes his rear fins.
The motions create a geometric nest
For the potential mate he wants to impress.
If the female fish finds
These sand designs fine,
She'll enter the center
And swim far away after the eggs are laid.
Males protect the eggs, and when they hatch,
They swim away from the nest, never to come back.

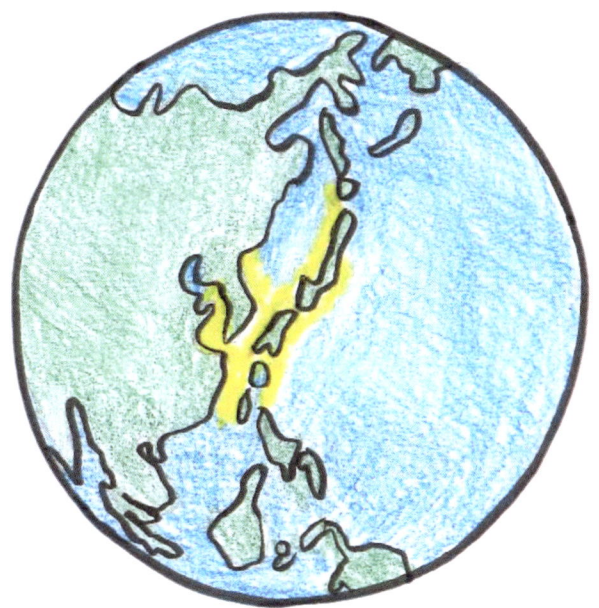

Sonation is what a manakin uses
To attract a mate with its own special music.
The male's ridged feathers and very dense bones
Rub together making a high-pitched tone.
Over 100 times per second! And if that's not enough,
He dances with hops and a backward strut.
She'll move from her perch to his if she likes the show,
Then fly off to lay eggs and watch her chicks grow.

Female hooded seals are known to swoon
When a male blows his nose up like a big red balloon.
The elastic nasal membranes and cavities
Are how he signals interest romantically.

Out his left nostril the red part inflates,
And makes sounds and noises when he gives it a shake.
Then the lady makes grunts, and in a circle she swims,
And gently makes contact, touching her nose to his.

Along the sandy banks of the Nile,
Basking and nesting, you'll find crocodiles.
A dominant male ROARS to scare other males out,
Making noises, blowing bubbles, hitting the water with his snout.
Flexing his body, rippling his flanks, creating sound waves,
Water vibrations tell the female he's headed her way.
If she swims off, the male is rejected,
But if they nuzzle jaws then she's interested.

When a penguin is hankerin' to not be alone,
It soon starts to search for a special smooth stone.
He'll look all around on the rocky beach ground -
And might even steal a pebble another penguin found!
A gift for a female, and if she accepts,
She'll use the stone to build a nest.
They build it together; then two eggs mom lays.
The chicks are raised in groups to stay warm on cold days.

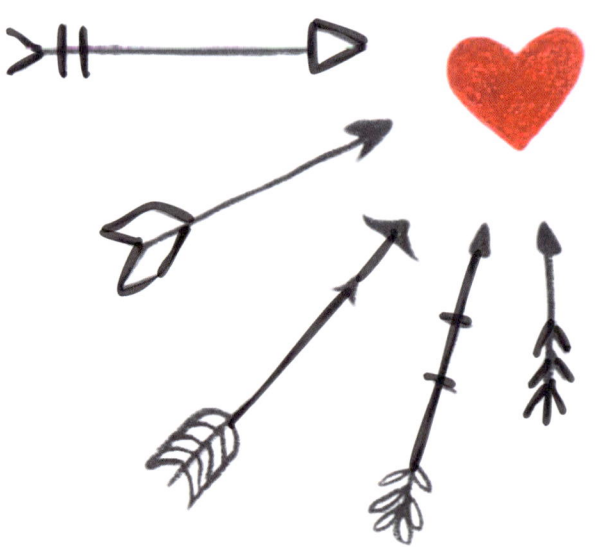

A saiga antelope
Is known to have a nose
Big, chunky and puffy.
When a buck has romantic hopes
He shakes it back and forth
Hoping a doe finds it lovely.
Then he chases the lady
Hoping that maybe she'll be wooed by his speed.
If she's not impressed, there's no need to stress,
He's got one more trip up his sleeve!
He puts a bush on his head,
And bleats out loud,
"Look at me now!"
Even though previously she turned him down,
Her feelings might change if she likes his crown.

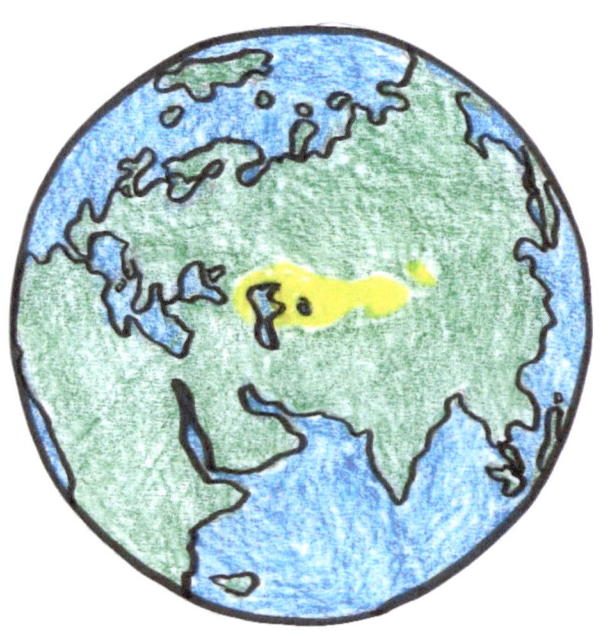

When a male peacock spider sees a female he wants,
He bounces his body and makes "rumble rumps" -
Vibrations the female can feel with her leg.
If that fails, there are two things he will do instead:
He'll flip up his flap with iridescent hues,
Reds and greens and yellows and blues.
They say it looks like a peacock tail,
Now it's time to dance and he must not fail.
The performance can last up to a whole hour.
If she doesn't accept, he might get devoured!

The satin bowerbird can build with the best,
So it makes a twig structure, but it's not for a nest.
It takes shells, and stones, and flower petal decorations,
bottlecaps and bones all in its creation.
We use red hearts to show we'll be true
But bowerbirds prefer trinkets that are blue.
When a female approaches to see what he's got,
He chirps and sings and dances and hops.
She'll visit a few to decide on her preference.
If she walks in the bower it's a sign of acceptance!

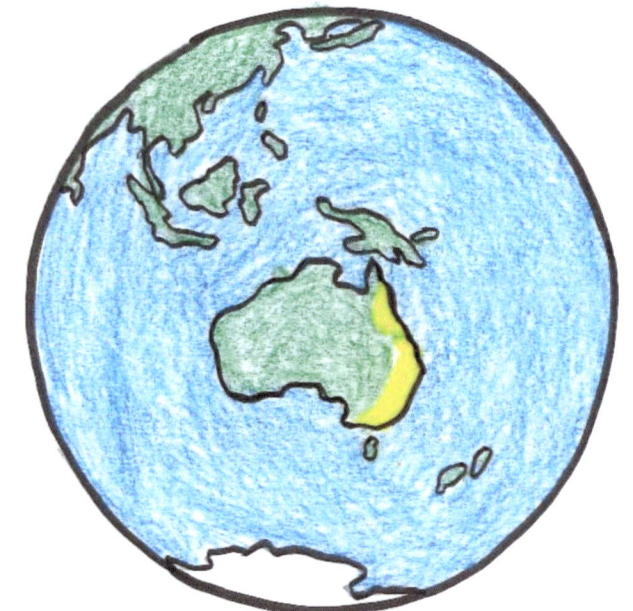

Female ostriches are very specific.
Examining male's health - to make sure it's terrific.
To test stamina, she'll run away and expect him to chase.
They do say that love can make your heart race!
When she slows, he'll dance around, and maybe drop to his knees,
As if to plead, "Give me your love please!"
If the female agrees, she'll flick her wing feathers
To let the male know that they can be together.

Female nursery web spiders' appetites are ferocious.
So the male brings a gift to distract as he approaches.
He wraps food with silk - a cricket or fly -
But he's a trickster, and sometimes the gift is a lie.
Taking pray he already ate, an exoskeleton or twig;
He wraps it up and hopes the female's fooled by the fib.
If she accepts the gift, then the male has a chance.
But if she finds out it's fake, there will be no romance.

We hope you enjoyed this Valentine's lesson
About the expressions of animals' affection.
These are just a few examples, there are so many more
In the animal kingdom, for you to explore!
Singing and dancing and building creations,
Maybe you'll find inspiration for your Valentine's celebration.
There's so much to learn from our animal friends!
And with that, dear reader, our book's at its end.

About The Authors

Eli and Tina have been together since 2018 and got married in 2023. Eli loves carrots, and Tina loves thrifting. When choosing a name for their publishing company, Thrifty Carrot Publishing was a natural choice!

They published their first story, *I Want to Go Outside*, in 2020. *Animals Send Valentines Too* is their second book. They are currently working on new books as they continue to get inspired. Eli has a talent for writing and rhyming, and Tina puts together ideas through illustrations.

Follow @thriftycarrotpublishing for future publications!
www.thriftycarrot.com

www.ingramcontent.com/pod-product-compliance

Lightning Source LLC
Chambersburg PA
CBRC09114103042G
4233TCB00010B/76